TOEBIRDS & WOODLICE

Toebirds & Woodlice

Leilanie Stewart

CONTENTS

Dedication xi

Toebirds & Woodlice 1

  1 - Ode To Childhood Dreams 2

  2 - Crustaceans And Arthropods 3

  3 - A Big Fat Waste Of Time 5

  4 - Forca 7

  5 - Conundrum 9

  6 - Don't Even Try To Do It Right 10

  7 - One From The Past 11

  8 - Shenanigans With The Mortals . . . 12

  9 - Pigs, Pink Pigs 13

  10 - A Malodorous Affair 14

  11 - Convolvulus Arvensis 16

  12 - Sock-it-to-me Football-head 17

  13 - Daddy-o 19

14 - Circles And Stripes	20
15 - Gums	22
16 - Triangle	23
Eye'm Watching You	24
17 - Semolina	25
18 - Ichigo Cow	27
19 - Rip Roaring Hatred	29
20 - Dancing Oddity	30
21 - Predator	31
22 - The Frivolous Earth	32
23 - 1066	33
24 - The Protagonist	34
25 - Greenwich Meridian	35
26 - The Last Act	36
27 - The Other Side Of Insects And Infidelity	38
28 - Cooking For Mr. Fishcake	40
29 - You Take It One Step Further	41
30 - Bloke In A Poke	43
31 - Is There Green In Everything?	44
32 - Cook Down Or Be Cooked	46

Frost Rings 47
33 - Bird's Eye View 48
34 - Blooming Scales 50
35 - Going Ape-shit With Frustration . . . 51
36 - Primordial Language 52
37 - Hey Fungus Eyes! Shot Put Your Own Bladder Into The Toilet 54
38 - Solitude On A Crooked Pavement . . 55
39 - Tinnitus 57
40 - Boil Me Plugs And Shut Your Trap! . . 58
41 - Bernard 59
42 - Pesky 60
43 - Pop An Olive In It 61
44 - The Relentlessness Of Fluff 62
45 - Cambrian Love 64
46 - Silverfish 65
47 - A Chill In The Blue 66
48 - Child Of Krakatoa 68
Snip It! 69
49 - Interplanetary Insanity 70
50 - Anatomically Modern 72

51 - Neanderthal	73
52 - Evapo-transpideration	75
53 - Optimist	76
54 - Sakana	77
55 - Crystallised Hope	78
56 - Pika Pika	79
57 - Dawdle	80
58 - Dandelion Fluff	82
59 - Sakana - The Return!	84
60 - Snakes	86
61 - Ms. Beachy-T	87
62 - Seven For A Secret	88
63 - Idiosyncrasies Of The Art Noveau	89
64 - What If...?	91
Legless	93
65 - The Geometric Venus	94
66 - Multifidus	96
67 - A Poignant Gander	98
68 - Caesarean Crap-pot	100
69 - The Simplicity Of All Things Far Away	101

70 - Fiddle-faddle For Thought	. . . . .	102
71 - Just Keep Going	. . . .	103
72 - Causality Of A Hopeless Dreamer	.	104
73 - An Abstract View	. . . .	106
74 - Macrofossil	. . . .	107
75 - Rot	. . . .	108
76 - Keep Out Of The Reach Of Children	. . . .	109
77 - Distractions	. . . .	111
78 - Salted Cod	. . . .	112
79 - No Room For Ruminants	. . . . . .	114
80 - My Perfect Land	. . . .	116
81 - Smackers	. . . .	117
82 - Idiot Eyeball	. . . .	118
83 - Waning Lyrical	. . . .	119
Figment	. . . .	120
About The Author	. . . .	121
Acknowledgements	. . . .	122

First published as a full 83 poem collection in 2023 by Leilanie Stewart

Published as a 20 poem pamphlet in 2012 by Leilanie Stewart

Toebirds and Woodlice Copyright © 2023 Leilanie Stewart

ISBN: 9781739952396

Cover design and internal artwork by Leilanie Stewart

The right of Leilanie Stewart to be identified as author of this work has been asserted in accordance with section 77 of the Copyright, Designs and Patents Act 1988

All rights reserved. No part of this book may be reproduced in any manner whatsoever without written permission except in the case of brief quotations embodied in critical articles and reviews.

Thank you for supporting independent publishing.

Website: www.leilaniestewart.com
F: facebook.com/leilaniestewartauthor
Twitter: @leilaniestewart
Instagram: @leilaniestewartauthor

Dedicated to all noodle-heads everywhere, but especially to the noodliest of all noodles, my two very own noodle-guys.

TOEBIRDS & WOODLICE

1

ODE TO CHILDHOOD DREAMS

Mira scotch-hotch
stole me money
and me right to breathe.

But I'm not a chunky bitch
ram me gaddow up yer ass
if you laugh at
me brown trews one more time.

Mira scotch-hotch
who's the sallow one now?

You don't fly
where the toebirds sail.

2

CRUSTACEANS AND ARTHROPODS

I peeled back the board
and saw woodlice
scuttling, crawling
I looked in my hair
and saw a centipede dangling
like a monkey from a liana.

But it was the woodlice
that bothered me.

I had to get rid of the woodlice–
I needed an amulet
a talisman.

If I were to put them on a net,
suspend them over sodium chloride,
they would leave in search of water–
a reflex action.

They only have crustacean brains
at the end of the day.

3

A BIG FAT WASTE OF TIME

I don't know whether
I'm coming
or going
or have already been
and returned
and am wearing
the t-shirt to prove it
or whether
I'd never been here
in the first place
or simply,
had come,
then vanished – just gone.

It's all irrelevant anyway
when I'm sitting here
talking to no one
in particular.

4

FORCA

You didn't tell me
you were a mermaid
you should have
I would have
treated you differently
I would have
worn my aqualung
I definitely
would have splashed around
in my little leopard-print speedos.

Why didn't you tell me
you were a mermaid?
I would have offered
to hold your shells
while you put on another bra.

We could have
eaten porpoises together
and whales.

These things are okay
if you have an excuse
if you're dating a mermaid.

5

CONUNDRUM

Once I had a cut
That formed a scab
Then I picked the scab
And made a fresh cut
That in a former life
Was once a cut
That someday will become a scab
And after that will form a scar
But if I happen to pick that scar
It'll ooze a fresh wound
That was once a cut
That will make a scab
And forever after, leave a scar.

6

DON'T EVEN TRY TO DO IT RIGHT

The gentle peaks and troughs
Of the undulating 'W'
Rise up to meet
The sedentary 'V'
Privy to its secret ruck.

And though the carcinogenic tide
May meet the lactic acid surge
It is kept there
In alembic
Yin and Yang will foil the purge.

7

ONE FROM THE PAST

Don't you fiddle
with your dib dib dibble
or I'll nib nib nibble
on your cock-a-leaky pie!

She cried, "Oi yoi yoi!"
to the sailor boy
with a Mo Mo eye
on a monkey-faced toy.

8

SHENANIGANS WITH THE MORTALS

Out of the aperture he came
his phantom limb a-clanging
trailing in wake of his wife
her woven womb hand-knitted.

And what a cacophony they made!
All flying sheep, not a stone unturned
let the living quake
and old Cernunnos marvel.

Excarnation is for fools!
A child's game to transcend rot
but deviants live by the laws of the ruthless
and Mercury lies redundant.

9

PIGS, PINK PIGS

Pigs on the edge of a precipice
all the bubbles are like snouts
and check out the tors on the top
just like curly tails.

The thing is, I see pigs everywhere
floating on cushions of marram grass.

Bacon flavoured, pig-shaped crisps
ridiculed, but the memory's intact
one was stolen, plump and round
a nicer treat than dog that night.

See over there by the photocopier?
Beware of pig-pork-pie.

10

A MALODOROUS AFFAIR

I was sitting thinking
stinking thoughts
my thoughts were ranking
oh, what am I saying?
Stinking, ranking,
what's the difference?
Indifference?
Or bureaucracy?

I'm as definite
as indefinite can be
or maybe inspired
hell, one of the two,
or all three,
or just wired

it would take you to be.
Independence?
Or hypocrisy?

11

CONVOLVULUS ARVENSIS

I reached down and realised
I have tits. They grew like
mountains of devil's lilies
snaking their way up
an adolescent fence.
Like Bindweed the
trumpets flowered,
invading the petals of youth.

Where did they come from?
But then, where did the hand
that touched them?

12

SOCK-IT-TO-ME FOOTBALL-HEAD

A man sat down next to me
on the bus, and I noticed
he had a gigantic round sphere
for a head.

It could have been a football—
it looked leathery enough.

I wanted to prod it,
just like I've always wanted
to prod plastic titties,
to see if they feel real
but I hesitated, in case

it was made
of papier mâché,
and filled with water.

Potentially, if it were to burst
it could ruin my new suit
and my interview shoes.

Despite this, I have to admit
I really wanted old football-head
to give me a Glasgow kiss
so that I could have felt
the sensation of hitting an airbag
in a car crash.

He didn't
and I was left
feeling deflated.

13

DADDY-O

Daddy-eight
Daddy-seven
Daddy-six
Daddy-five
Daddy-four
Daddy-three
Daddy-two
Daddy-one
Daddy-o

Daddy-no
legs.

14

CIRCLES AND STRIPES

They're coming for me
the grey lines
I saw the first one yesterday,
heard the metallic clink
like an iron bar against a drainpipe
but the mind can't think straight.

I see the grey lines
crisscrossed like a lattice
through my inner eye
but behind the eyelids, closed,
there is no refuge
black circles fill the gaps in between.

I saw this coming
once upon an idealistic time
yet it doesn't make life easier now.

15

GUMS

Darkness with a pair of teeth
Teeth on a vast wall of black
Gnashers hung in billowy nothingness
Dentures bared, all cavity and gums
Show me your canines
and I'll show you my velvety noir.

16

TRIANGLE

Pointy on top
three sides pristine
arrogant manner
naïve as a child
cold-blooded, cold-hearted
busy to the eye
truculent as a bulldog on heat
splendid as a frozen lake
incongruous in a bathroom
smells like rose
sounds like a wind chime
looks like a bird's beak

Triangle.

EYE'M WATCHING YOU

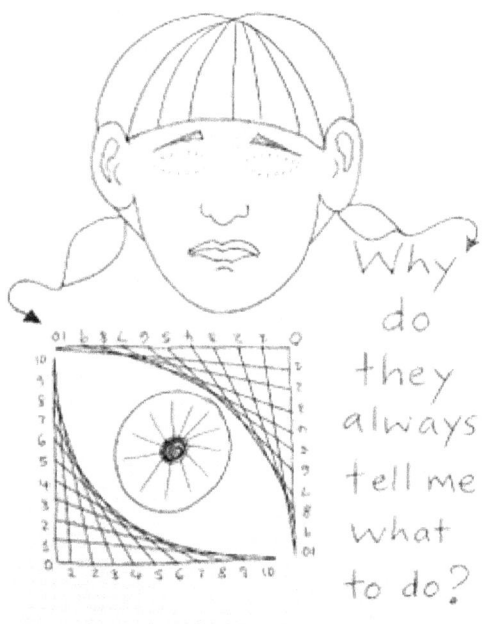

Why do they always tell me what to do?

17

SEMOLINA

Spirulina
      Spirulina
           Spirulina
Semolina
      Spirulina
Semolina

Semolina,
yum, yum

Semolina,
if you're clean
then it'll mean
you never get it

Just forget it,
I was thinking
Salmonella,

Oh my!

18

ICHIGO COW

Cow ca-dow!
They say how now
but I don't trust
that furrowed brow.

Cow ca-dong!
Am I wrong?
Cos I won't listen
to your inferior song.

Cow ca-dile!
Megalomaniac style,
but I see through
your inferior smile.

Cow ca-boom!
Doom and gloom,
in this strawberry field
for only one, there's room.

19

RIP ROARING HATRED

When I see him, it's like
my eyeballs are engorged with poison
and my brain is distended, hanging,
from my skull like a tongue.

What's the fuss about this baboon?
He's nowt but a snake charmer...

...and my patience is wearing thin.

20

DANCING ODDITY

Clouds or jacks
Clouds or jacks
A ghost of a jack
Dancing on bubbles
A herd of eggs
Wrapped in a hanky
Concave eggs
Where do teardrops go?

21

PREDATOR

You said you like
my shape
and
you want to
know me a bit further
but I think you are
a pervert.

22

THE FRIVOLOUS EARTH

Isn't it funny
how life works out?
Let's take a moment
to laugh at it.

I don't want to talk
of blue skies and love
but of poikilothermic wrestling matches
and bickering bulrushes,

cos that to me
is the general feel
of what life's all about.

23

1066

1066 was the year
of the Battle of Hastings
John De Courcy and all that
or didn't you listen in History class?
I've a right cheek to talk
It's all I remember
ask me another and I'll make something up.

1066 came and went and left it's trace
in the minds of those who nod,
never to be seen or heard of again,
for we all know
time changes
at 10 fifty nine.

24

THE PROTAGONIST

Red satin stalactites
hanging from my knees
count them if you dare.

Gold tasselled centipedes
eating through the carpet
of them you should beware.

Turquoise philanderer
flying through the sky
making people stare.

Purple-headed snake-worms
on a roundabout
Don't you even care?

25

GREENWICH MERIDIAN

It's a line
It's a silly-split
It's a trombone,
It's a tombola,
It's a trombola
at a tombola
filled with,
filled with–
vinegar.

26

THE LAST ACT

It's made of rubber
but nobody told me this
and I didn't figure it out
I just knew it.

I'm afraid to open it up
Who knows what I might reveal,
might unearth?
What if a giant cockroach leapt at me?

Where does this stuff come from?
From a feisty geyser,
or the turmoil of a merciless heart?
And what happens next?
What's the half life?

We could put it on a throne
bestow it with beautiful jewels
but time would laugh in the face of vanity.

I can hear it
moving like clockwork
predict malfunctions
syncretism dies
just like the cycle of all things in the end.

27

THE OTHER SIDE OF INSECTS AND INFIDELITY

All I saw
were white stripes on black
before I died.

Then,
I was swimming in a field of green
with turtles
and pink tacos.

The sun didn't set on me that day,
not does acid rain on me now.

How can I describe heaven?

Bliss is like butt cheeks on bike seats
Why the need?
When cars can take us
down the bypass of life.

28

COOKING FOR MR. FISHCAKE

I'm putting the pork in the oven now
Mr. Fishcake C
I say, I'm putting the pork in the oven now
Mr. Fishcake, Fishcake C
But the foil won't rip, you see
Mr. Fishcake C
So, what's a girl to do?
When it's all in the mind for me.

29

YOU TAKE IT ONE STEP FURTHER

Squeeze it
make it pop
drain the poison
tear the hooks off
pull the legs off
burn it.

And now?
See the proglottids?
Kick them!
Smash them!
Stamp on them all.

I've had enough
rip the wings off
wrench the teeth out
snap off the proboscis
see if I care.

It's evil
It's evil
hack of its head
or it'll never stop.

30

BLOKE IN A POKE

Bloke in a poke

Well, he's not without arms
or without legs

Oh, now look, I've got yoke
on my fingers and dress

Will he give me a poke?

With his long wafer stick
or his chocolatey flake?

Yes, his creamy-fit flake.

31

IS THERE GREEN IN EVERYTHING?

Is there green in everything?
You turn it one way and it's pink
but on the whole, it's actually silver.

Is there symmetry in everything?
You see it face on and where's the centre?
How can I trust it,
when I don't know where to focus?

Is there good in everything?
You think you know it and feel placated
but when it bites, it's fibreglass
on the metaconscious.

Is there freedom in everything?
You think there's individuality
though if you lag behind
the shoal will leave without you.

32

COOK DOWN OR BE COOKED

I've cooked your goose
but the goose ain't down
it's climbing up that steep old hill.

You're a miserable son-of-a-bitch at times
though I've gotta say it,
you've got spirit.

If you really must insist
on fighting the fight
then I'll cook up a storm
and bring you down

after the tornado.

FROST RINGS

33

BIRD'S EYE VIEW

Grey pigeon
on a live wire
watching the bubbles
go up through the water
like hiccups in a baby's chest
and contemplating the dew
on a blade of grass
after pondering the hills
on the moon.

What does it matter anyway?
says the bird.

Take flight my friend,
take flight.

With the brilliance
of the sunrise.

34

BLOOMING SCALES

Swirling, swirling, swirling corks
Swirling, swirling, swirling corks
Cauliflowers blooming in a field
One half, one half, trit-trot, trit-trot,
stop.

On your toes
one mistake
and the scales will come to get you
soldering iron at the ready
blast that verruca dead.

35

GOING APE-SHIT WITH FRUSTRATION

Don't boil over!
You boiling over bunch of baboons
for the drills are coming
the drills, the drills!

The blue and white drills
are attacking the sinks
and the babes
and the minks.

36

PRIMORDIAL LANGUAGE

Under the cover of darkness
the words slipped out of my head
like a Spanish dancer,
a mist of innocent frivolity
echo rebounding off bone.

And yet there was no trace,
no visible form,
vowels like ribbons of fire
leaping off an inert tongue.

They say walls carry the burden
though flesh, it carries none.

Where do words go?
When they're said and heard
but not remembered
sounds uttered
under the decadent cloak of midnight
are gone.

Words said before,
spoken today,
disappear with the primordial flow
transcend planes mid-sentence.

How can we catch
what we cannot see?

37

HEY FUNGUS EYES! SHOT PUT YOUR OWN BLADDER INTO THE TOILET

Pissywhips
piddled on the seat.

How irritating is it
to get wee in your socks?

I'll urinate on your bloated corpse
if you'll die in front of me.

38

SOLITUDE ON A CROOKED PAVEMENT

Kidney-bean man
walking along on his s-shaped feet
round and round in circles.

Round and round in circles
round and round in black and white
Kidney-bean man
stumbled in figure eights.

Boomerang-man
looking with his button eyes
at the oblong flappers.

Oblong
obtuse
refuse
dripping down the drain...

39

TINNITUS

Tinnitus
Tinnitus
Tinny-tinny-tinny-tuss.

Tinnitus
Thin it was
When it took a swipe at us.

Devil of the fens came nigh,
Feasted on my flesh, cos I,
Catch all the demons flying by.

40

BOIL ME PLUGS AND SHUT YOUR TRAP!

I think you sprayed
too much hairspray on my brain
if it had a mouth
it would call you a bastard
but I'm here to do the honours
Would you get me a skateboard?
So I can ride into the kitchen
and dance a jig with the teapot
for all blackened creatures of the hearth
know that you're the one
who blocked the drain.

41

BERNARD

Bernard was Bernie
or Barry
maybe Billy?

He was tallish
not thin
but not stout
and not white.

Nor black; wait,
Caucasian
not Asian,
contradiction–

Okay, I'll admit it
I'm wrong.

42

PESKY

The books are like piano keys
white and black and white and black
the buzzing can stop now
waiting– waiting–
the tapping might end now
I hate it– hate it–

The connection is severed
it's over for real.

43

POP AN OLIVE IN IT

It is as it is
A small one, tis
A hot old wiz
And for your biz
It makes you fizz,
Mizz–

Juniper.

44

THE RELENTLESSNESS OF FLUFF

The fluff won't stop
it keeps coming and coming.

It really won't stop
it's just coming and coming.

The harder I pull
it keeps coming, just coming.

Look at my fingers
they're strumming and strumming.

Best get out your knife
for it's coming, it's coming.

You can't cut it off
the war drum is drumming.

45

CAMBRIAN LOVE

Look at me with invertebrate eyes
as we swim along in Palaeozoic seas
and create mud-casts of love in the sand.

You, who are made of primordial soup
and I, with my superior brain
and our love, as bright as a binary star,

in this young world of ours.

46

SILVERFISH

Silverfish. Slivers of. Shreds of. Wood. Fragments of. Termites reject. Silverfish. Darting. In. And out. Carpets. And holes. And silverfish.

47

A CHILL IN THE BLUE

I thought I caught a blister
a sister
a chilblain
I made my woollen cushion
to keep the chills away.

I wrapped my scarf round tighter
and higher
and brighter
I leaned towards the heater
and painted myself blue.

I painted myself aqua
and blue
all through
I sank into the furniture
and blended with the school.

I wore my scarf of turquoise
and my cardigan of blue
I blended with the heater
and felt a little blister
a sister pass me by.

I pulled my scarf round tighter
and scooched my backside higher
upon my noodle-cushion
where the furniture was drier
then I sank into the blue.

I sank into the blue
with my coffee mug a-steaming
and the radiator colour
matched the aqua
of my book.

A blister came a-creeping
a-sniffing
a-weeping
I sipped my mug of aqua
and felt the chill pass through.

48

CHILD OF KRAKATOA

In 1883
she said to me–
run for it, child!
Anak, anak,
I'm going to Krak

Krakatoa
gonna blowa
gotta goa.

SNIP IT!

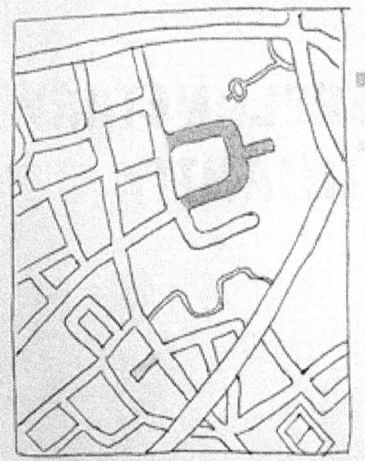

49

INTERPLANETARY INSANITY

Painted
into the grain
sealed by the vertical lines
released from your creosote breath
it comes much easier now
the continuity unbroken.

But still–
shivering, flowing,
it's almost obscene.

If it shuts
they'll crack
the power enthrals
the fear pursues.

Touch it
just once – just this once
staring through those golden liquid globes
the elliptical orbit
cuts the heart.

50

ANATOMICALLY MODERN

It comes of its own free mind
and it's fully formed–
I can't stop it.

It might have been brewing for centuries
a mya, perhaps,
so who am I to argue with that?

If you change the order of even one part:
adenine/guanine/cytosine/thyamine/urasil
it's all over for good.

51

NEANDERTHAL

Nean
Neany-derth
Neany-derthal
Nean-snake-man.

Coal
Coal-a-can't
Coalacanth
Coelacanth.

Coal-a-snake
Coal-snake-man
Neany-coal
Coaly-nean-man.

Coal-a-snake
Neany-fish
Homo-man
Nean-a-fish-man.

52

EVAPO-TRANSPIDERATION

Spidery raindrops
arachnid clouds
little spiders get bigger
through a silken web of sky.

Are spiders and raindrops
born of the same lunacy?
Water alone is deceived.

I won't condone the hairy throughfall
you percolating fiends
for Minerva knows the truth
of all eight-legged evaporated hearts.

53

OPTIMIST

The only way to gain anything
is to lose everything
'cause if you have nothing
your teacup is empty.

I like my teacup
with milk and no sugar,
or rather the tea
which you'll see is half full.

54

SAKANA

Fish like sand
fish like ribbons
silk fish
fish like water
gloop gloop fish
smack smack fish
floating fish
whirlpool fish
fish that dance
fins on fish
flapping fish
vertical fish
fish that dive
spit-stones fish
five fish
guilt-trip fish.

55

CRYSTALLISED HOPE

See how they swoop?
passionate bombs
tracks in the glare
hastily dissipated
milky whitewash
an array of encrusted trees
riparian flow
of knives through my heart
I realise I must succumb
schizo temperament
is beyond my control.

56

PIKA PIKA

A multi-faceted crystal
when hung in the eyes of a house
will break the bad feng-shui.

In the uterus of an empty place
it'll grow, filling the void
with the nectar of new energy.

The sun will not be siphoned off
The light will not be shared.

57

DAWDLE

I've tried many times
to compose this poem
in my head, in the bath,
while I sat on the loo,
or busied about doing
mindless chores.

Yet, still
it seems to evade
being captured by the lasso
that I've constructed
from my curling letters of ink.

I'll wiggle my fingers
for a bit longer,
and hopefully
my mind will catch up.

58

DANDELION FLUFF

I think
a dandelion seed
may have gone up my nose
it might have lodged itself
in my brain
even now as we speak
it could be starting
the germination
of a whole new breed
of dandelion children
inside my head

Soon
my hair will turn yellow,
festooned
with the yellow petals
that define me
as a weed
taking over the earth.

59

SAKANA – THE RETURN!

Freak out fish
only two

Orange fish
reddish hue

Noisy fish
glub, glub, glub

Happy fish
in a tub

Cloudy tank
fish don't care

Brainy fish
pretty rare

Rival fish
struggle quick

In-out fish
what's the trick?

60

SNAKES

A hand is a hand
a foot is a foot
but hands and feet
can never reach the same place.

What's the goal on the horizon?
I can't decipher it
with all the monkeys cackling
in my ear.

Snakes are like static
tune them in
or drain them from your wretched brain.

61

MS. BEACHY-T

Bumpety-bumpty surface,
but offended when they say bumpettes.

Soft as peaches and cream,
a life lived with no regrets.

Relaxed,
but austere at first glance.

Spins a maelstrom of colour
like a Spanish dance.

Not the type for a one-night stand
lives a hedonistic life of sun, sea and sand.

62

SEVEN FOR A SECRET

Magpie
A Madam-pie
One for sorrow not today
Wings tucked under on the shelf
Once saw shiny objects fly,
But now feet buried in thick dust
Mr Black-and-white-and-pointy
Not your day today my friend
Only glue for asphalt eye, and
Wadding for that rounded breast.

63

IDIOSYNCRASIES OF THE ART NOVEAU

They're lined up in rows
but still uneven
It offends the eyes, the mind, the soul
The tip of the iceberg–
Brown and red – maybe yellow
you'd be a fool to argue
instead,
let the chain of thought slide down
the flaky guttering
into the bowels of the–
dug-out,
hollowed-out,
empty chimney.

It's a vessel, only a container
for part of that which is dead
and free
still, the angles left
on the hollow shell are irregular
and it torments, even blisters
a life fragmented.

Don't even try to understand
what has already been
and passed,
emitted into the ether
like a puff of smoke.

64

WHAT IF...?

My neuroses
have kept me up
all night.

Like,

What if
a car crashed
through my window?

Or,

What if
the fire alarm
didn't go off?

Then,

carbon monoxide
carcinogenic fumes
would waft in.

A night wasted,
sleep
wasted.

What if?
What if?

What if.

LEGLESS

65

THE GEOMETRIC VENUS

I was born in the earth, the mud gave
birth to a beauty of celestial mirth,
there's no other waist of
comparable girth, a
sacrificial figurine
for the
firth.

With my shapely breasts and
vulva so wide, I'm a symbol
of fertility and pride, not
men nor gods will hide
their hopes and fears
in me they confide
and answer their
prayers I do, not
chide. The geo-
metric Venus
will bide and
give her
answer
on the
tide.

66

MULTIFIDUS

I've always wanted to write a poem
tucking the word multifidus
into a stanza somewhere.
I'm telling you straight up,
so you don't think I'm pretentious.

It's the whole point of my poem,
I'll admit it
and I haven't even got
to what it means yet.

Please don't think I'm insulting your intelligence,
or your reflexes.
You've probably known all along what it means,
or reached for the dictionary
before I could say jack-shit.

And all this time while I've been thinking,
writing,
my multifidus is slowly going dead,
feeling sorry for itself,
that for eons it hasn't had
a dorsal fin to keep it alive.

67

A POIGNANT GANDER

I've always wanted to write a poem
tucking the word multifidus
into a stanza somewhere.
I'm telling you straight up,
so you don't think I'm pretentious.

It's the whole point of my poem,
I'll admit it
and I haven't even got
to what it means yet.

Please don't think I'm insulting your intelligence,
or your reflexes.
You've probably known all along what it means,
or reached for the dictionary
before I could say jack-shit.

And all this time while I've been thinking, writing,
my multifidus is slowly going dead,
feeling sorry for itself,
that for eons it hasn't had
a dorsal fin to keep it alive.

68

CAESAREAN CRAP-POT

I said "God-damn!"
when the paper was hot
but you weren't bloody listening,
got your eyes
on them olives
Now, I'm the boy to tell you
when there's brown on white
takes two to tango
but only one to take the pen.

69

THE SIMPLICITY OF ALL THINGS FAR AWAY

She said she was going to the shop with me
She was going to the shop with me
She was going, she was going
She was gone. Gone
And yet she wasn't at the shop with me
The door was in front of me
A big oak door with brown and cream
And did I scream?
Hell, yes!
And I banged and banged, but
Still the shop was there
And I was here.

70

FIDDLE-FADDLE FOR THOUGHT

It's back to basics
"Back to basics?"
Whatever does that mean?
When yer at home?
Bird shit on ye?
Thought not, or nowt thought?
Yer all the same
under the surface
jus' the stitching looks different.

71

JUST KEEP GOING

It's juicy
If I squeeze it
will it turn around?
and bite my finger?

If I squeeze it
will it pop?

Will I be left
with a skin-sack
as an aftermath?

72

CAUSALITY OF A HOPELESS DREAMER

I touched it – it floated
on an eddy of gold dust.

I cracked a rib
as it flittered away.

I followed,
it led me astray down a path.

Where possums played
in Mulberry trees.

I pushed on into candyfloss clouds
it ascended into a fissure of light.

I watched through the V in my fingers
I closed my eyes and reached.

73

AN ABSTRACT VIEW

This orange rubber
is growing too much

An occasional shockwave
rocks this hump

There are prickles, tickles,
then saltwater flows

And a pain where red
is swelled shut to meet red

What can be done about it anyway?
It's part of this world, and without it,

Nothing.

74

MACROFOSSIL

Quercus
What can you tell me of ziggurats?
Oh, how you'll never see
It's so one-sided.

Tephra
What would you know of cuneiform?
The varves are too young,
Much too young.

Coleoptera
They're coming and they're sensitive
They'll lay the rest to bed
In your fields. Your ponds. Your cities.

75

ROT

I have a little patch of gangrene
on my soul
right above the astral umbilical cord
I tried to pick it off
but it spread,
it happened around the time
my goldfish died, one by one
I suppose if I'm reincarnated
I'll end up being a melanin-rich fungus
growing on the reactor
of Chernobyl.

76

KEEP OUT OF THE REACH OF CHILDREN

Wash your hands after use
Don't get it in your eyes
Get that bloody dog out of here!

And that swan while you're at it,
Oh, my mistake – it's the shape of the bottle.
Well, hurry up – the mushrooms are sprouting!

I said to use it only here,
And here, and here
Aren't you listening?

What a palaver, carry on.
We haven't got all day you know.

There's seriously more muscle in my cock
than you've got in the whole of your forearm.

Now look what you've done!
You've whipped it into a right old mess
and stained the carpet,
wonderful!

77

DISTRACTIONS

I'm crossing them out
I'm doing corrections
line by line,
giving injections
changing the meaning
adding deflections
altering tone–
I meant inflections
tell me the orders
I need directions
I'm at a standstill
amidst retractions.

78

SALTED COD

I wanted to swim with you
in oceans of aquamarine
in our own idyllic paradise.

We could have leaped ahead of ships,
leading others through coral reefs
into a world of fathomless beauty.

But you strayed into shallow shores
and stagnant lagoons
I tried to lead you out, though it was hopeless.

Now all that is left for me to do
is string you up,
dry you out on a hook like the rest.

I'll keep you for a morsel on a rainy day
and trust me,
I won't feel bad about it.

79

NO ROOM FOR RUMINANTS

I'm feeling a bit
hard done by today
because I don't have four stomachs.

Whenever I eat a big meal
I feel bloated – I could honestly do
with three extra stomachs to churn the food.

I wouldn't even mind
chewing the cud, so long as
it was a pizza-crust, or a tasty rice ball.

And while I'm on the topic
a diastema would be nice
to grind all the grainy foods.

Why do I have to be
Ruminantly challenged?
When we all know—

Modern cattle
eat grains anyway,
instead of the grass they're supposed to have.

# 80

MY PERFECT LAND

There's a city that stands like a teapot
if you're dandering down by the bay
and looking ahead over vinyl dunes
beyond cotton wool tufts of hay.

It glitters so bright in the sunset
that it tames the waning tide
and the mountains are left in a jealous furore
though the buffalos well up with pride.

81

SMACKERS

A pair of lips
on a sea of skin

What's the point?

82

IDIOT EYEBALL

Idiot eyeball
cast over a drumlin nose
and yet the waves of grass keep coming
their gentle peaks and troughs
placate my tepid mind.

83

WANING LYRICAL

These are the lyrics
to the song of all I've got
left in me
I've been squeezed like a lemon
you wouldn't believe I even had a flavour
but I assure you I do
and it'll be back tomorrow.

FIGMENT

I no longer exist in the conventional sense of the word.

I am simply a figment of my own imagination

Leilanie Stewart is an author and poet from Belfast, Northern Ireland. Her writing confronts the nature of self; her novels feature main characters on a dark psychological journey who have a crisis of identity and create a new sense of being. She began writing for publication while working as an English teacher in Japan, a career pathway that has influenced themes in her writing. Her former career as an Archaeologist has also inspired her writing and she has incorporated elements of archaeology and mythology into both her fiction and poetry.

In addition to promoting her own work, Leilanie runs Bindweed Magazine, a creative writing literary journal with her writer husband, Joseph Robert. Aside from publishing pursuits, Leilanie enjoys spending time with her husband and their lively literary lad, a voracious reader of books featuring creatures of the deep.

ACKNOWLEDGEMENTS

Thank you to my hubby and editor for putting the polish on these poems from way back when they were first published in magazines and anthologies.

Acknowledgements are due to the editors of the following publications in which some of these poems were first published: The Fat Damsel; Mad Swirl; Dead Snakes; The Open End; Morphrog; Jellyfish Whispers and Erbacce.